Shine Through the Shadows

A Woman's Story of Trauma, Redemption, and the God Who Never Let Go

Salina Watson

Copyright © 2025 by Salina Watson

All rights reserved. No part of this book may be reproduced, stored in a retrieval system, or transmitted in any form or by any means; electronic, mechanical, photocopy, recording, or otherwise; without the prior written permission of the publisher, except in the case of brief quotations embodied in critical articles or reviews.

Printed in the United States of America

First Edition

Independently published

ISBN: 9798280137752

Important Note

This book is a work of nonfiction based on the author's personal memories, beliefs, and lived experiences. Events are recounted to the best of the author's recollection. However, the passage of time, trauma, and personal perspective may have impacted how certain events are remembered or interpreted.

To protect the privacy of individuals, names, identifying details, and locations have been changed or omitted. Some scenes, dialogue, and timelines have been recreated, combined, or altered for clarity and narrative flow.

Some characters are composites, and certain timelines have been adjusted for clarity and privacy.

Any resemblance to actual persons, living or dead, beyond the author's direct experience, is purely coincidental and unintentional.

The author does not make any claims regarding the accuracy of other individuals' actions, intentions, or experiences and assumes no responsibility for how others interpret or respond to the contents of this book. Any mention of a person, relationship, or event is not intended to cause harm, defame, or assign blame.

This book is not intended as a substitute for professional advice, whether medical, legal, psychological, or spiritual. Readers are encouraged to seek qualified guidance when needed.

The purpose of this work is to share one woman's story of survival, healing, and faith, and to offer hope to others walking through darkness. The author has written with the intention of honoring her truth and glorifying God.

Dedication

To Marilyn Walker,

We were young women starting life on our own; roommates in a tiny one-bedroom bungalow we could barely afford, and friends long before we had titles or timelines.

We then got to watch each other raise families. You were a free spirit, full of grace, and always able to forgive with ease. You soaked in the beauty of life, even when it was hard.

As cancer took your body, you still spoke life into mine. You told me to write this book, and I finally did.

Though you're no longer here to read it, your fingerprints are all over these pages.

"See you on the flip side."

Foreword

I received an email from my aunt:

"This was a communion talk that your uncle gave. Hope it helps with your story."

I asked for permission to one day include this; his telling of my beginning; as the foreword to the book I'm writing about my life.

The Resurrection of Salina

"The closest I've ever come to witnessing a resurrection was the night my sister-in-law called to say her baby had stopped breathing.

My brother and I rushed to her house and arrived well ahead of the ambulance. The home was in such disrepair that there was no electricity or light in the baby's room. My sister-in-law was too afraid to return to her lifeless child.

I had to feel my way through the darkness.

Find the crib.

Find the baby.

Find my way back to the light.

We laid the blue-skinned infant across a forearm, tilted her head back into the palm of a hand, and shouted resuscitation steps at each other, watching desperately for signs of breath.

Just as I lowered my head to begin rescue breathing, her chest rose ever so slightly

and Salina started coming back to life.

She didn't regain consciousness right away, but her breathing became shallow and steady until the paramedics arrived and transported her to the hospital.

Salina eventually came home, fitted with a heart monitor.

And despite a couple more heart-stopping episodes, her heart would go on to become one of the strongest in our family.

There are resurrections like this happening all over the world today.

Some of us have neglected the new life given to us the day of our baptism, and we need to return to the Light. Some of us need to clear our airways and remember the confession that washed our sins away. Some of us need to breathe new life into our commitment, our following, our honoring of Christ.

Ezekiel 37:10

"So, I prophesied as He commanded me, and the breath came into them, and they lived, and stood upon their feet; an exceedingly great army."

Jesus has fitted each of us with heart monitors.

And His Church is an exceeding great army of brothers and sisters,

those who help us exercise our hearts,

warn us when our spirits grow weak,

and revive our memory of Jesus… and the sacrifice that gives us the longest of lives."

Introduction

What a beautiful little girl; long curly brown hair, emerald eyes, and an enormous heart for others. No one warned her she would face a life of relentless suffering. From the very beginning, the enemy was after me. And strangely, that has always been what pushed me to survive.

Even now, at 44 years old, I don't fully know what God is doing with my story. Though I believe, without a doubt, that He will use it for good. That's why the conviction to write it down has never left me. Over the years, people have spoken the same words to me: "You should write a book." I think it's finally time.

Why did it take me so long? I wish I had an answer. Maybe because I kept waiting for the story to feel finished. I've realized; however, some stories never tie up neatly. Life doesn't suddenly get easy, and I won't reach some perfect moment of "arrival." My testimony isn't what I've overcome. It's what I carry. Not in a "poor me" kind of way, but as a light in someone else's darkness.

Joy has always been my fiercest battle, but I refuse to let the enemy steal it. Even if he succeeds in destroying my physical body one day, this fight isn't just about me. It's about breaking chains for the generations to follow.

This morning, I found out my sibling is back in prison. I learned through a text, not to me, but to my 13-year-old daughter, from my mother. A woman who was never a mother to me and failed again as a grandmother. When I looked up my sister's mugshot, her inmate number memorized, I saw a hollow version of the girl I once knew. Soulless eyes, the heartbreak of addiction written across her face.

Strangely, I felt relief. Not because of where she is, but because I know she's no longer out there, lost and running. Of course, I feel grief. For what could've been, for the sister I love, for the life she could have chosen. But I also know this: God can do miracles. I've seen Him do it in me. My prayer is that she cries out to Him, that she lets Him rescue her. But she still must make the choice.

Her story isn't for me to tell, but it has shaped mine.

This book has taken so long because I feared it was all too much. That *I* was too much. I didn't want to spill a pile of heavy stories onto the page just for the sake of trauma. If that's all it was, no one would pick it back up after the first few pages. But this story isn't just hard, it's holy. It's the proof that you can survive things that should have killed you. And not just survive, be reborn.

If you've ever felt like it's too much… that you're invisible, forgotten, or broken beyond repair… this is for you. I wrote it with shaking hands and a prayer that it would find you. That it would remind you: you're not alone, and your wounds don't have to be wasted.

Table of Contents:

Important Note
Dedication
Foreword
Introduction
Chapter One – Normal Never Was
Chapter Two – The Night We Escaped
Chapter Three – Spiraling
Chapter Four – Stolen
Chapter Five – Building Something
Chapter Six – The Call That Changed Everything
Chapter Seven – Wanting More
Chapter Eight – Trained By Trauma
Chapter Nine – The Breaking
Chapter Ten – Letting Go
Chapter Eleven – A Birthday, a Bar, and a Boy
Chapter Twelve – Blood Doesn't Mean Bond
Chapter Thirteen – When Peace Feels Suspicious
Chapter Fourteen – The Wedding That Was Ours
Chapter Fifteen – Becoming Me
Chapter Sixteen – The House Faith Built
Chapter Seventeen – When the Body Speaks
Chapter Eighteen – Rescuer, Wounded
Chapter Nineteen – Starting Again
Chapter Twenty – What Helped Me Heal
Appendix – Mentioned Conditions Explained
Author Bio
Acknowledgements
Dear Reader
Let's Stay Connected

Chapter One – Normal Never Was

Like most children, I was naturally happy and playful. I was blind to the difficulties all around me; it was normal. I didn't know any different.

I grew up in a small town in Oregon, surrounded by vivid green forests and water. I shared a tiny bedroom in a run-down single-wide trailer, with my older sister. We're Irish twins, only months apart, and we had a lot of time together before the others came along. That trailer had orange shag carpet, wood-paneled walls, and the smell of old must and sadness baked into it. We were dirt poor, though I didn't really understand what that meant at the time.

The trailer park may have been nice once, but by then, it was tired. Our patch of yard sat beside a small creek. We'd catch frogs, salamanders, and tadpoles like they were treasure. There was a burn barrel out back; I don't understand why burning trash was normal, but it was. No recycling bins. Just fire and smoke.

My dad worked graveyard shifts. That meant he slept most of the day. My mom had married him when she was 16; he was barely older. She stayed home. It wasn't until years later that she picked up work at a fast-food place.

There were stretches when we didn't have running water or electricity. Often, we were locked in our bedroom, told not to come out; even to use the bathroom. I didn't know then what I know now: the adults were using drugs. I just knew we had to be quiet. So quiet, in fact, that we sometimes had to relieve ourselves in the room. The stench lingered, and I can't fathom how they didn't notice; or didn't care.

We would sneak out when we could, pressing the bedroom door in the opposite direction so it would open, even while locked. If we got to the bathroom, we were allowed only two squares of toilet paper. Two. If we managed to go undetected, we would skip the TP entirely to leave no trace behind and sneak back into our room.

Food was scarce, and we survived on the kindness of churches, food banks, and government programs. If you have ever had powdered milk or sliced into that giant block of government "cheese," you know. It wasn't really cheese. Maybe "cheese product," at best.

When my brother was born, things shifted. My dad lit up; he finally had a son. His pride in my brother made my sister and I feel invisible. Still, I loved being a big sister. I felt this fierce sense of protection over him. Three years later, my youngest sister was born, and I became mama bird to two baby birds.

By then, my mom had started working outside the home. My dad slept during the day, and we were left to our own devices. We were expected to be "quiet as a church mouse." We basically lived outside when we could, riding bikes, playing in the river (far too dangerous, looking back), and creating our own worlds in the dirt and grass.

School became my sanctuary. I loved it. I was on the honor roll and part of the Talented and Gifted program. Music, reading, and writing came naturally to me. I played the clarinet, and later the oboe, bass clarinet, and bassoon.

I practiced for hours and hours at home, moving my fingers across the pads and blowing air through the reed without making a sound. My sad songs of silence. Yet it was my way of surviving the noise of everything else.

Books transported me far away from reality. I devoured them, sometimes too advanced for my age. I was reading my mother's Stephen King and V.C. Andrews books in third grade, which now seems insane, but it was normal to me. I also loved to sing. I sang at church where I felt safe, and softly in the car; until my dad would suddenly turn down the radio just to hear and tease me. It stayed with me. To this day, I have to fight through fear and doubt every time I sing, even while leading worship.

He often mocked my fears, which left a lasting mark. I hated heights, so he would pretend to drive off cliffs or swerve toward the edge of a bridge just to see me panic. He once dangled my baby sister over a bridge by one arm, the river raging below. We swam at the place just beneath the bridge there in the summers. I've done years of exposure therapy on myself to conquer that fear, but it continues to surface; especially if I am not the one driving.

At school, I felt seen. My band teachers believed in me. I took first chair in third grade and kept it all the way through school. Looking back, I think they knew what I was going through. When money was tight, they found a way to cover band camp or gifted me "old" instruments, which were actually beautiful, expensive pieces. They never made me feel like a charity case. They let me be invisible in a world where invisibility kept me safe.

They saw me; the misfit girl in secondhand clothes, with bruises she tried to hide, and a hunger that wasn't only about food; and they gave me dignity.

Back then, I didn't know how strange my life was. I didn't realize that not everyone had to be silent to stay safe. That not everyone was afraid of the door creaking, or footsteps approaching down the hallway. I thought this was how life worked. It would take years to unlearn that kind of survival. But even then, something inside me kept whispering:

"You were made for more."

Chapter 1 Reflection Questions – Childhood Reality

1. What memories from your childhood feel "normal" now but were actually rooted in survival?

2. Who or what made you feel safe, seen, or capable when the world around you felt unstable?

3. If you could speak to your younger self in that environment, what would you want them to know?

Chapter Two – The Night We Escaped

I can still feel the gravel digging into my knees... the taste of blood in my mouth.

We were ducked behind the car, breathing hard, trying not to make a sound. My body was running on pure adrenaline; I couldn't yet feel the bruises from earlier that day. I had run to the bathroom to hide, but he got there before I could lock the door. He barreled in like a monster. His hands, big, meaty, and full of rage, landed over and over again. At one point, I hit the toilet so hard it knocked the wind out of me.

Now I was trying to get my siblings into the backseat. We had left the car door cracked enough to avoid the cabin light coming on, just enough to avoid the click that would give us away. Everyone was accounted for, except the baby. She was still inside with my parents.

Then it happened.

The front door burst open. My mom, bloodied and frantic, holding the baby tight in her arms. She was nearly blind without her glasses, which had been knocked from her face. Behind her, my father. He physically overpowered her and pulled her back inside.

The baby screamed. My heart stopped.

I had planned for this night. We had practiced for years. Our "in case of emergency" plan; if she didn't come back out, we were to run.

But I couldn't move. We were frozen. Quiet tears streamed down our faces as we listened to the sounds of the struggle inside. Doors slammed. Things were being broken, and I could hear wails of agony. I started to lose hope.

Then, another burst; the door flung open again. She made it. She had fought him off, hard. Later, I would learn she nearly bit his finger off in the struggle. She threw herself and the baby into the car. He wasn't far behind.

We backed out of the driveway at full speed. He chased after us, barefoot, bloodied, and enraged. A wall of muscle and steroid-fueled insanity. He looked possessed.

That night should have been the end of us. But instead, it became the beginning of a new life.

It wasn't the first time he had beaten my mom, but it was the first time she left for good. I'm proud of her for that.

What followed was chaos and hiding. We stayed with my mom's friends, bounced around, eventually landing in a battered women's shelter in a nearby town. It was the first time I saw other families like ours. The first time I felt less alone.

But he didn't let go. Not for years. He found us more than once; waiting on the couch of our home when we walked in, showing up unannounced, as if he owned us. Even when we thought we had vanished.

One time, I was tricked into babysitting for one of his new girl-friends. He had taken one of those little flyers I made with the tear-off tabs and called me like a stranger. I didn't know where I was until it was too late. If I called my mom for help, I would have made everything so much worse.

He and his girlfriend came home after several hours, drunk and fighting, and I was trapped. Her kids were sleeping.

He finally stormed out. She didn't. She stayed and slit her wrists in front of me.

I don't remember how I got home. I just know I survived.

My mom eventually remarried. My stepfather was more stable, and they had another child; over a decade younger than me. He got a different version of her. The softer, more present version. The one who was trying to do it right this time.

He never knew what we knew. He never saw what we saw.

He had his own room. His own toys. Clean clothes. Birthday parties. He got the mom we dreamed of having.

It was obvious, she favored him. She favored both the boys, really. We girls were reminders. In her eyes, we were defiant, rebellious, ungrateful. We didn't make her feel needed.

Her love often felt conditional, offered only when it served her.

I learned young not to need anyone. Not to rely on love or help or comfort. And I became really good at pretending I didn't want it.

It shows up now as hyper-independence. As the relentless drive to succeed. As the belief that if I just work hard enough, no one can ever hurt me again.

She once said to me, "You make me feel like trash."

I told her the truth: "I don't have control over how you choose to feel."

That night behind the car wasn't the end of my childhood, it was the start of me learning how to fight for my life. I didn't always get it right, but I never stopped fighting.

Chapter 2 Reflection Questions – Breaking the Cycle

1. What "escape plans" have you had—either real or emotional—to survive hard seasons?

2. What patterns or relationships from your upbringing have you had to unlearn or release to protect your peace?

3. Is there a moment in your life where fear gave way to courage? What happened?

Chapter Three – Spiraling

We moved to Arizona because I was spiraling, and because my sister and I had gotten good at running.

I was only twelve when I started numbing the pain. Alcohol and cigarettes came first, but they quickly gave way to harder things. By thirteen, I had tried marijuana, cocaine, LSD, mushrooms, peyote, PCP, meth, ecstasy, GHB… even nitrous oxide and anything else I could inhale. Pills, powders, patches; you name it. I didn't care what it was or what it did. If it made me forget, I'd take it.

It's a miracle I'm alive today.

Arizona was supposed to be a fresh start. A reset. But it felt like punishment. I was ripped away from the only people who believed in me; my teachers, my band director, the little pieces of normal I clung to back in Oregon.

I had been set up for a full ride to Juilliard. That dream shattered the second we moved. Our new town was tiny and insular. They didn't care for outsiders, and I showed up already labeled a problem, guilty by association with my older sister. She was a grade ahead of me and had already made her mark, so teachers decided who I was before I even walked through the door.

"You will never amount to anything."

No teacher should ever speak those words.

And yet, decades later, they still echo in my mind; uninvited, but unforgettable.

I went from honor roll to failing almost overnight.

So, I quit. Not on paper, but in my heart. I stopped going to class. I gave up music. I silenced the one thing that gave me a voice.

Juilliard was no longer an option. My future felt gone.

We lived with my grandmother, my mother's mother, which was ironic, given how strained their relationship had always been. Still, it was shelter.

At least, for a while.

I became too much for even her to handle. My punishment? Exile. I was sent to live in a tent in the backyard.

When the snow came, I moved to the tool shed.

There was no heat. No bathroom. No insulation. I was like an animal; only allowed inside the house when invited. I existed on the edges of everyone else's lives.

I found safer places in friends' homes. I don't think they ever realized how much they saved me. If I was going to be locked out anyway, I might as well plan for it. I learned who would let me crash on the couch. Who would offer me a hot meal. Who would treat me like a human being.

Even in my rebellion, I was still desperate for love.

I had already been cutting. But the pain wasn't enough anymore.

One night, I slashed my wrists. It wasn't a cry for help; it was a moment of pure hopelessness. But as soon as I did it, I regretted it. I panicked and wrapped the wounds myself. Covered them up. Hid the evidence.

I still have a scar on my wrist. Faint, but there. A reminder that even at my lowest, something inside me still wanted to live.

My mom reported me as a runaway. Not because she was afraid for me, but to save face. To make it look like she cared.

That landed me in the back of a police car, cuffed, on my way to juvenile detention.

I don't remember how long I stayed, but it was long enough. Long enough to realize I never wanted to end up locked away like my father had been, in and out of jail all my life.

I wanted different. I simply didn't know how to find it.

My older sister had also dropped out of high school and gone to Job Corps. She was in Utah, thriving. She had gotten out. Maybe I could, too.

I enrolled at the Tucson Job Corps, planning to study culinary arts. I have always enjoyed cooking. It gave me joy, even in the darkest seasons.

But when I got there, I found out the program was gone.

I was sixteen years old. Five hours from anyone I knew. Alone.

I could've left. But something told me to stay.

And maybe, for the first time, that was the beginning of a choice that would point me toward healing.

I didn't know it then, but staying, *choosing to stay*, was the start of a shift.

The pain didn't stop. The mistakes didn't disappear. But a tiny part of me, buried under layers of hurt, had started to hope again.

Chapter 3 Reflection Questions – Spiraling and Searching

1. When did you first start numbing pain instead of facing it? What did you use to cope?

2. Have you ever lost a part of your identity—like music, creativity, or joy—because of trauma or transition?

3. What's one time you surprised yourself by surviving something you didn't think you could?

Chapter Four – Stolen

I stayed.

Even after learning the culinary program was gone, I stayed at Job Corps. Something inside me; maybe desperation, maybe a flicker of hope; told me not to give up. I chose a new vocational path: Electronic Assembly.

It wasn't glamorous, but it gave me purpose. I learned to read schematics, solder components, build circuits. I liked the structure, the quiet focus of it. I wasn't planning a career so much as building a way out.

But the darkness didn't disappear just because I changed locations.

I brought it with me.

The party had already started when I walked into the motel room.

Loud music. Booze. Pills. Too many people. I don't even remember how I got there, only that I didn't want to feel anymore. Not the shame. Not the memories. Not the hole inside me.

So, I drank. Took whatever they handed me.

At some point, everything went fuzzy.

I remember flashes; someone stroking my hair. A voice whispering in my ear. Laughter. Pain. Then blackness.

When I came to, I was surrounded by bodies. Dozens of teenagers were passed out. The floor was sticky with spilled beer. The room reeked of cigarettes. I found my clothes. My bag. I stepped carefully, trying not to wake anyone, even though I wanted to scream.

I didn't remember everything. But I remembered enough to know what had happened.

I had been passed around.

Too drugged to say no. Too gone to fight back. Treated like I was nothing.

I didn't tell anyone.

Who would believe me? I had taken the drugs. I had gotten in the car. I had gone to the party.

That's what shame does; it convinces you that the worst thing that happened to you was somehow your fault.

I shoved it down.

I walked back into the center dorms as if nothing had happened. Took a shower. Showed up for class. Kept breathing.

But inside, something broke.

I didn't feel like a person anymore.

Years later, I would come to understand what really happened that night.

That being too intoxicated to consent is not consent.

That what they did was rape.

That I wasn't weak; I was victimized.

That I wasn't worthless; I was wounded.

And that healing was possible, even from this.

But back then, all I felt was used.

I thought, this is just what happens to girls like me.

Girls with broken homes. Girls with colorful pasts.

Girls with no one to protect them.

That night laid the foundation for a painful pattern: confusing attention for love…seeking affection through sex, accepting crumbs from men who saw me as disposable.

I had never seen what a healthy relationship looked like. I had no blueprint.

I was clueless, just trying to survive.

I wish I could go back and hold that girl. Tell her it wasn't her fault. That her worth wasn't lost in that room. That she was still loved, still chosen, still redeemable.

But I can't go back.

Instead, I'm writing this now; for the girl I was… and maybe for someone else who is carrying shame that doesn't belong to them.

You are not what happened to you.

Chapter 4 Reflection Questions – Stolen Innocence

1. Have you ever felt ashamed for something that wasn't your fault? What would it look like to release that shame today?

2. What messages did you internalize about your worth after being hurt, rejected, or used?

3. If you could speak to a younger version of yourself in a vulnerable moment, what would you say to remind them of their value?

Chapter Five – Building Something

I graduated.

Despite everything; the trauma, the chaos, the self-destruction; I finished my vocational training. I obtained my GED. I earned a certificate in Electronic Assembly and walked away with something no one could take from me.

It wasn't glamorous, but it was *mine*.

I moved into an apartment with roommates, got two jobs, and enrolled in college using a Pell Grant. I was barely scraping by, but I was proud. For once, I was building something that looked like a life.

One woman gave me a chance; no experience, no résumé; just trust. She hired me at a bed and breakfast near campus. I worked mornings, serving breakfast and cleaning rooms. Able to attend classes in between duties. In the evenings, I picked up shifts at restaurants. I made sure I had at least one free hot meal a day.

My schedule was heavy, but I didn't care. I had direction. I had bills to pay. I had goals.

I thought I wanted to be a pharmacist. Not because I was passionate about medicine, but because it sounded like a "real" career. Something stable. Something that made money. Something I could be proud of.

But I wasn't ready for the academic grind… or the weight of doing it alone. I was still drinking too much, still partying, still carrying a mountain of unresolved pain. I was going to class by day and numbing by night. Eventually, it caught up with me.

I dropped out.

Not because I didn't care, but because I didn't know how to ask for help. And if I'm being honest, I didn't have anyone to even ask.

Years later, I'd go back to school again, this time for interior design.

I was in my early twenties, still trying to find myself, still working food service jobs. Then the unexpected happened: I landed a part-time leasing agent role at a brand-new apartment complex.

It didn't seem like much at the time. Weekends only. Answering phones and showing units. But I loved it. I was good at it.

My experience in hospitality helped me get my foot in the door. So did the fact that my boyfriend's aunt worked for the company. This town has always been about who you know.

That leasing job would end up changing the entire trajectory of my life.

I realized I had a choice: I could keep bouncing between service jobs and late nights… or I could build a career.

I chose the harder path.

I went all in.

I knew I didn't have the formal education others did, but I could outwork anyone. I absorbed everything I could about property management. I volunteered for the tasks no one wanted. I learned by doing. I listened. I asked questions. I hustled.

Slowly, the party girl began to fade.

The drinking didn't disappear. But ambition took the front seat.

For the first time, I saw a future I could shape with my own hands.

But just when I thought things were finally settling...

Everything flipped upside down.

This chapter of my life taught me two things:

I am capable of building something from *nothing*...

And even in the rebuilding, the past will always find a way to surface, until you're ready to face it.

Chapter 5 Reflection Questions – Building Something

1. What job, role, or opportunity helped you begin rebuilding your confidence after a hard season?

2. Have you ever walked away from something safe in faith—without a backup plan? What did you learn?

3. What dreams have been buried by survival mode that you may be ready to revisit?

Chapter Six – The Call That Changed Everything

"Hello?"

The voice on the other end was my aunt. I hadn't spoken to her in years. I was confused. How did she know where I worked?

She didn't waste time.

"Nina, I'm so sorry to have to tell you this… your dad died two days ago."

The world went hazy.

I drove fast, music blasting; Evanescence pouring out of the stereo like it could hold me together. My family had eventually relocated nearby. I ended up at my mom's house, still too stunned to speak. She didn't even need an explanation when she opened the door. She already knew.

Before I returned my aunt's message, I had called my mom asking why she thought she would be reaching out. She had shrugged and said, "Maybe your dad finally died." She wasn't even being cruel, just resigned. Maybe a little relieved.

And maybe I was too.

He died homeless.

They found his body early in the morning, propped up against a fence in a public park. A jogger discovered him. I'm sure this memory has lingered with them, and I feel a deep sadness on their behalf.

At first, I thought that was the end of the story. But later, grampa told me something else; someone had informed him that my dad hadn't actually died at the park. There were rumors that he may have died somewhere else and was later moved, possibly to avoid complications. I don't know for certain, but the idea haunted me.

That hit harder than the death itself.

Even in death, my father was *discarded*.

The autopsy revealed what we already suspected: heroin, opiates, alcohol. A toxic mix of substances that his body couldn't survive. After everything; after all the destruction, the violence, the years of silence and shadows; this was how it ended.

Alone. Propped against the fence. Left like trash.

It shouldn't have surprised me. And yet, it did.

I spiraled.

The grief was complicated. How do you mourn someone who terrified you? How do you cry for a man who used his strength to crush everything around him?

And yet, part of me loved him.

That's the cruel irony of trauma, it makes you grieve who you needed them to be, not who they were."

I drank more than ever. I was reckless. I somehow managed to hold onto my job, but school was another story. I couldn't focus.

Couldn't finish. I was too close to the end to quit, but I quit anyway.

I went back to the coast for his funeral. My aunt and uncle paid for the plane ticket. They picked me up in Portland and drove me to the small town where my dad grew up. My grandparents still lived there; in the same house I remembered from childhood.

The moment I walked in, I was flooded with memories. The tree house in the front yard. The garage that smelled like tools and sawdust. My grampa's handmade myrtle wood furniture. The safety I used to feel in his arms.

He had always been kind to me. I wonder now if he knew. If he sensed the violence his son was capable of and tried to make up for it in quiet ways.

Those days at the beach were some of the only good memories I had with my dad. When others were around, he pretended to be normal. I got a glimpse of who he could have been.

And now, it was over.

But something unexpected happened at the funeral.

For the first time, my extended family knew the truth. And instead of pretending, we talked about it. We cried together. We shared stories. We started to heal.

Not from his death.

From his life.

It wasn't losing him that hurt the most. It was knowing I had already lost him a long time ago.

But somehow, in his absence, I found a little piece of freedom. I no longer had to look over my shoulder. Worried that he would one day just show up again unannounced.

Chapter 6 Reflection Questions – Loss and Legacy

1. What grief in your life has been complicated or layered—hard to process because of the pain that came before the loss?

2. How have you seen God use even painful endings to create space for healing or new beginnings?

3. What's one thing you've learned about yourself by facing death, whether literal or symbolic?

Chapter Seven – Wanting More

I had recently ended an engagement with a man who turned out to be someone I didn't recognize.

What he had done behind my back was vile. Not just betrayal, but deeply troubling, possibly criminal. And it wasn't just personal; it bled into my professional life. He had crossed a line with my employer, and somehow, I was still standing.

I don't know how I kept that job. I should have lost everything. But the truth came out, and they believed me. They saw that I wasn't part of it.

Still, it shook me to my core.

That same year, I was diagnosed with early-stage cervical cancer.

The treatments were aggressive. The conversations were terrifying. I was young, too young to be talking about whether I'd ever be able to carry a child.

That fear sat in my chest like a stone.

So did the loneliness.

I moved in with my brother, not because it was convenient, but because I didn't feel safe alone.

That man I left? He didn't take rejection very well.

He stalked me.

He showed up where I worked. Parked inside the gates of my apartment complex. Sat outside real estate school late at night, waiting.

He drove beside me on the road, pretending it was a coincidence.

It was calculated. Constant. Creepy.

Eventually, I got a restraining order. I started carrying concealed. I learned how to shoot. Got comfortable with a firearm. It wasn't about violence; it was about reclaiming a sense of power.

And sadly, this wasn't even the first time I'd been stalked.

My track record with men was… not great.

After that breakup, I decided: No more.

I didn't want another short-term, toxic relationship. I wanted something real. Marriage. Family. A partner who saw me.

But before I could have that, I knew I needed to be alone. To face myself. To heal.

So, I did something different.

One night, I sat down and wrote a list of everything I wanted in a future partner. I was oddly specific; right down to the kind of work he did, the way he made me feel, even what he drove.

When I read it out loud to my brother, he laughed.

"I know that guy," he said.

I rolled my eyes. "Yeah, right."

"No, I'm serious," he insisted. "You described one of my friends."

Given my brother's own dysfunctional history, I wasn't exactly enthusiastic about that idea. But he was persistent. He orchestrated it so that this friend would give him a ride home from work… so we could meet.

Sneaky. But effective.

And honestly? I was surprised.

He wasn't what I expected. There was something solid about him. Calm. Grounded. Different.

We started dating.

Three years later, we got married.

We bought our first house. Had two children. Built what looked like a real family.

I thought I had finally done something right. Something normal.

But I should've known by now, because it looks good on the outside, doesn't mean it's safe on the inside.

I was chasing love. Wholeness. Redemption.

But I hadn't yet learned that real love doesn't require you to earn it.

And real safety doesn't come from control, it comes from truth.

Chapter 7 Reflection Questions – The List and the Leap

1. What patterns have you recognized in your past relationships that you no longer want to repeat?

2. Have you ever written down what you truly want in a partner, friend, or community? If not, what would that list include today?

3. What would it mean for you to believe you deserve a love that chooses you?

Chapter Eight – Trained By Trauma

Not long after we got married and began building a life together, I found myself in an unexpected moment that tested everything I had ever learned about fear, instinct, and survival.

While I was eight months pregnant with my first child, I was working at the office. What started as a seemingly normal day took a terrifying turn when I suddenly heard gunfire. Multiple rounds, right outside my office window. I hit the ground instinctively.

My employer, not registering the sound, started walking toward the window to investigate. I immediately told her to get down.

Because of everything I've been through, I have come to understand how I respond in crisis. Time slows. My senses sharpen. I can think clearly and act quickly.

What used to be sheer survival instinct has since been refined through formal training.

I reached into my purse, pulled out my firearm, and army-crawled across the floor to wedge a chair against the door. Our only point of entry.

Then I crawled to my boss, shielding both of us behind her desk, the farthest spot from the exterior wall. I grabbed the key fob and triggered the security alarm. All of this happened in seconds.

Still unaware of what was happening, my boss yelled, "You have a GUN?!" Then, "Who ARE you?!!" She was staunchly anti-gun and didn't know that I carried concealed anyway.

However, in that moment, her fear shifted to gratitude. From that day on, she started calling me "Pregnant Rambo." It's hilarious to hear her retell the story.

We were stuck in the building for several hours after closing while police investigated. The office was in a rough part of town, a known hotspot in the area's meth epidemic.

According to the police, our parking lot had been the site of a drug deal gone bad. One man apparently tried to burn the other, which turned into a shootout right outside our windows.

The gunfire continued even as they sped away, bullets flying into the neighborhood.

My employer's car was hit, but luckily mine was in one piece.

God protected us that day. I had been getting ready to leave for a showing appointment. If I had been outside, or already in my car, this could have been an entirely different ending.

Chapter Eight Reflection Questions – Calm in the Crossfire

1. When have you been surprised by your own strength or clarity in a crisis? What did that moment reveal about you?

2. Have your past traumas shaped how you respond to fear or danger today—for better or worse?

3. What training, instinct, or preparation has God built in you that could be used to protect or help others?

Chapter Nine – The Breaking

He wouldn't leave.

Even after I found what was on his computer; things that broke my heart and shattered my image of the life we were building; he refused to move out.

So, I *left*.

I packed up the kids and found a small rental. It wasn't much, but it was mine. A place to breathe. A place to begin again.

The kids were one and three.

I felt like a failure.

Christmas was coming, and I didn't have money. I scraped together enough for the tiniest artificial tree—barely taller than my toddler. I set it on our little dining table and told myself it was enough.

Then I got sick.

It started with a cough. Turned into pneumonia. I was exhausted, running on fumes with no help. No one to call. No one to lean on. I couldn't bring myself to tell friends the full story. The shame kept me quiet.

I pushed through the pain until I couldn't anymore.

The coughing got so bad it broke a rib. I tried taking half a pain pill, but it made me vomit, sending shocks of pain through my chest and back.

Have you ever thrown up with pneumonia and a broken rib?

It felt like dying.

I was struggling to get around with the kids. Lifting them in and out of the tub or car seats. Picking them up when they needed me. Everything became so much harder.

Their father had a hunting trip planned. I begged him to please stay and help. He went anyway.

And then, Christmas Eve came.

The kids were with their dad. I was alone in the rental. Curled up in pain, listening to the silence.

The shame was deafening.

This wasn't how it was supposed to be. I had gone through hell to get here; for what? A shattered marriage? A dollar-store tree? A cough that cracked my ribs? Wine as my only companion?

I opened another bottle. I tried to distract myself with TV. Nothing worked.

The voices got louder. Not audible voices, but thoughts.

What's the point?

You're too much.

You'll never be enough.

They would be better off without you.

The thoughts were not mine, but they were in my head; clear, cruel, convincing.

That scared me more than anything.

I prayed; something I hadn't done in a long time.

Not the folded-hands kind of prayer.

I screamed inside my soul.

Why?!

Why has my life been so damn hard?

Why do I have to carry all this?

I let it all out; ugly, furious, broken.

And then… silence.

Not the haunting kind. The holy kind.

I didn't hear an answer. But I felt something shift. The fact that I was still breathing… meant something.

Eventually, I passed out.

And when I woke up, I was still here.

That night didn't fix everything. But it did prove one thing:

The darkness did not win.

Not that night.

Not then.

Not ever.

Chapter 9 Reflection Questions – Christmas Alone

1. Have you ever felt completely alone—physically, emotionally, or spiritually? What helped you survive that moment?

2. What lies has the enemy whispered to you in your lowest moments, and how can you start replacing them with truth?

3. When was the last time you cried out to God—not perfectly, but honestly? What happened?

Chapter Ten – Letting Go

I didn't believe in divorce; that's why I waited until I was 28 to marry. I thought time and maturity would protect me from failure.

But here I was—betrayed.

And though I wasn't sure I could forgive him; I gave him time. I don't want promises, I want proof. Show me, through your actions, that I matter.

I gave him three months.

Looking back, it wouldn't have taken much; a little effort. A heartfelt pursuit. Even a whisper of change.

I could have forced it by caving. But I didn't want another cycle. I wanted love; the kind that treasures, not tolerates. The kind that chooses, not settles.

I still believed in marriage, but I believed in myself more. Three months passed. Nothing changed.

So, I filed for divorce.

Just to prove I was done; I joined a dating app.

Not because I was ready; but because I was angry. I wanted him to feel even a fraction of the hurt he left behind.

Seven long months later, it was official. I was divorced… and left in financial ruin.

Chapter 10 Reflection Questions – Treasured, Not Tolerated

1. What boundaries have you had to set—or still need to set—to protect your heart and your healing?

2. When was a time you chose dignity over desperation, even though it was hard?

3. What do you believe about your worth today, and what do you want to believe going forward?

Chapter Eleven – A Birthday, a Bar, and a Boy

Who knew I would meet the *love of my life* only a week later?

We started talking on the phone. No pressure, no drama; easy conversation. But I was terrified. I didn't trust myself. I couldn't afford another mistake.

I asked God for wisdom. Discernment. Patience. Please don't let me rush into anything.

Because truthfully, I hadn't joined the dating app for the right reasons. I was still hurting; angry and reeling from all my ex had put me through.

When this new guy and I discovered we shared the same astrological sign (both Libras) I asked when his birthday was.

He said, "October 18."

I froze.

That's my birthday.

It might not sound like much, but in my last two serious relationships, both men forgot my special day.

Once? Fine. Twice? It starts to feel personal; like you're not even worth remembering.

But this guy? He couldn't possibly forget, unless he lost his mind. I told him, okay, sir… I'll let you take me out.

We met for dinner.

The conversation flowed like we had known each other for years. We talked for hours until the restaurant closed, then ended up at a nearby pool hall. When that closed too, we called it a night.

It was a random Tuesday, the only day that week we both didn't have our kids.

He kissed me before I left, and I floated all the way home. One night in, and I already wanted a second.

On that first night, I told him clearly: I will never get married again.

He didn't argue.

He had his own mess; an ex-spouse, a brutal custody battle, wounds that hadn't healed.

We dated for three years before he worked up the courage to propose.

Somewhere in that chapter, we opened our home to my family. Again.

My mother had moved away again, then returned to Arizona after her divorce and needed a place to stay. With her came my youngest brother. Then my other brother and younger sister joined us, fresh out of prison.

We were trying to help. Again. But like before, it backfired. I felt misled and taken advantage of.

It got to be too much.

When my mom first left the state, my sister was still a child, and she didn't even know they'd moved. She came home to an empty house at only 13 or 14. I had taken her in then. Became her legal guardian. Tried to love her through it.

She ran again. And again.

Eventually, I had to let them all go.

We reclaimed our home and asked everyone to leave.

Of course, I was painted as the villain. *"Perfect Nina"* strikes again.

But I've learned that protecting your peace will always upset the people who profit from your chaos.

And through all this, my boyfriend wanted to marry me.

He asked my mom and stepdad for permission.

They said no.

Panicked, he realized he had to propose immediately before one of them ruined the surprise.

I was in Phoenix for a training with a new job. He came to visit. We spent the day by the pool, had dinner, and returned to the hotel room. I had no idea he had been a nervous wreck all day.

He was running out of time, sweating every phone call I got, worried they would blow his cover.

We had a little inside joke. When one of us said "I love you," the other would respond, "Prove it."

That night, he said I love you. I echoed prove it.

And when I turned around; he was on one knee, holding a ring.

I said yes. Loudly. Without hesitation.

And for once, I felt chosen.

Not as a backup plan. Not as a project.

But as a partner.

This wasn't the kind of love that swept me off my feet.

It was the kind that held my hand through the fire.

And finally… it was a love that stayed.

Chapter 11 Reflection Questions – A Birthday and a Beginning

1. Have you ever experienced a moment that felt like divine confirmation—like God was giving you a little wink or nudge forward?

2. What fears or beliefs have made you hesitant to receive new love, even when it's healthy?

3. What would it look like to trust again—not perfectly, but courageously?

Chapter Twelve – Blood Doesn't Mean Bond

We bent over backward for family; until we broke.

We stayed connected to both sides, showing up, extending grace, overlooking the jabs and silence, the exclusion and one-sided effort.

Because… family is everything, right?

Yeah, okay.

Eventually, we learned: just because someone is related to you doesn't mean they get a free pass to mistreat you.

Our families made it clear; they weren't invested. Not in us. Not in our kids. They excluded them, made no effort to connect, and somehow expected us to always be the ones to reach out.

Over time, we had enough.

We started setting boundaries, real ones.

We decided: we will no longer tolerate behavior from anyone that dishonors our peace. Blood or not.

That space eventually grew into no contact with some. Including my mother.

For the first time in my life, I felt free.

Free from being the family scapegoat. Free from her manipulations. Free from the cold jealousy she carried like a shield.

We faced unexpected challenges during our fostering journey, including a legal process that required me to share my history under oath. Some of that involved difficult family dynamics.

I told the state what I had been through; the years of abuse I endured under her roof. She may not have inflicted the worst of the harm, but she watched it happen. She let it happen. For over a decade.

Her actions felt deeper than bruises; petty cruelty, emotional games, cutting comments, simmering envy. It all added up.

I think seeing me create good from the wreckage of my past threatened her. I became everything she may have never had the chance to be.

How dare I grow.

How dare I heal.

The thing is, I wanted a family. Desperately.

I wasn't looking for perfection. Not picture-perfect holidays, just connection. Something that even slightly resembled the love I saw on TV growing up.

But I've come to accept… I'll have to create that myself.

Some people won't grow. Some won't change. And if protecting my peace makes me the villain in their story—so be it.

I miss my siblings.

But I love my sanity more.

Chapter 12 Reflection Questions – Blood vs. Boundaries

1. Have you ever had to set boundaries with family to protect your peace or your children? What did that cost—and what did it free you from?

2. In what ways have you grown into someone your past self (or family) never expected?

3. How do you respond when you're misunderstood by those closest to you—and what would it look like to release their opinions?

Chapter Thirteen – When Peace Feels Suspicious

Blended families are hard, and no one tells you exactly how hard.

We walked through it all, courtrooms, accusations, and investigations.

There was even a claim of molestation against one of our kids; completely unfounded, of course, but terrifying all the same. We endured multiple DCS visits and investigations. Endless legal drama. Character assassinations from people who didn't care how much they hurt the children involved, so long as they could hurt us.

One parent seemed determined to disrupt our peace.

She ended her marriage. Started a new life with a new identity, no issue there. But somehow, the idea of him moving forward with us was too much.

It felt like she wanted to destroy what we had.

And honestly? I still *don't* understand why.

We endured until the kids were grown. Did our best to protect them. Survived what may have broken most people.

And when it was finally over… there was silence. The children were now adults and that severed any tie to her for good.

Peace.

But it felt suspicious. Foreign. Like maybe we should brace for another storm.

That's what trauma does; it trains your nervous system to live in survival mode. When things are calm, you're still flinching.

Sometimes peace is uncomfortable.

It feels like waiting for the other shoe to drop.

We're learning to live in the quiet, without fearing it.

Chapter 13 Reflection Questions – Blending and Breaking

1. What unexpected battles have come with trying to build a healthy family, marriage, or home?

2. Have you ever been falsely accused or unfairly judged? How did that shape you?

3. What would it mean for you to live in peace—even if your nervous system is still waiting for the next blow?

Chapter Fourteen – The Wedding That Was Ours

We decided not to invite the madness.

We had both already done the big, expensive weddings—and hated it. The stress. The tension. The drama.

We wanted different.

So, we eloped.

No guests. No pressure. Us and the ocean.

When the cruise coordinator asked about the guest list, planner, and wedding party, we smiled. "Just us."

They gave us a full cake and champagne anyway. It was sweet; absurd, hilarious, and absolutely perfect.

Ten days in the Caribbean. No one else to please. No one else to manage. Simply love, peace, sunshine, and saltwater.

The ocean is my happy place.

But before the cruise, we had some things to make right.

We had been attending church together for a couple years. I sang in the choir. He led a small group. During our marriage prep, our pastor lovingly brought up what we had already felt convicted about; we were living together unmarried.

We had justified it. The wedding is already planned. We're committed.

But deep down, we *knew* better.

We didn't want to just talk about values. We wanted to live them. We then decided to get married sooner; only the two of us, our kids, and a small ceremony at church.

It felt right.

We decided to include both of our mothers. This was before we went no contact. And, of course, that came with its own drama.

My mom invited everyone out to dinner after; and then left us with the check.

Later, when we watched the ceremony video, we caught my mother-in-law on camera mumbling (loudly) about the pastor using my husband's nickname instead of his given name during the vows.

Okay, really? You go by your middle name. Why does it matter?

We laughed about it later. It was either that or cry.

And still—it was beautiful.

All four kids witnessed our families becoming one. We showed them what love looks like when it fights for peace, for growth, for something deeper.

We didn't need a crowd.

We simply needed each other.

And the courage to start fresh, for real this time.

Chapter 14 Reflection Questions – Just Us

1. When was the last time you chose joy over people-pleasing? What did it feel like?

2. Have you ever had to redefine what a "perfect day" or "perfect family" means for you?

3. What's one area of your life where you're being invited to simplify—and savor?

Chapter Fifteen – Becoming Me

We had to figure out how to build a healthy relationship from scratch. Neither of us had great examples growing up—marriage, parenting, finances… we were winging it.

We started our life together in financial ruin; both of us dragging debt from previous relationships. But I was determined. I've always been willing to work. I would take on two jobs if I had to. I was all in on anything that made our children feel safe and loved.

I stayed in property management, even took a leap into a new company and role. It felt like a fresh start; exciting and new.

Five months later, I walked out.

No job lined up. No safety net. Just faith that it would work out.

And it did.

I cried to a friend, unsure of what I had done; and she offered me a job on the spot. I started right away.

It was bittersweet. I thought I had found a way out of the niche I had built for myself, but I landed right back where I started: property management. It wasn't terrible, but I was beyond burned out. My heart wasn't in it anymore. And it was starting to show.

That season cracked the door open to something new.

Around that time, I started a health program. I was tired of the weight and tired of not recognizing myself in the mirror. I wanted to feel strong. To feel beautiful on my wedding day.

And I did. I lost 100 pounds.

For the first time in ages, I felt incredible.

My coach noticed that people were constantly asking what I was doing. *"You're sending me so many referrals,"* she said. *"Why don't you coach them?"*

At first, I laughed it off. I was exhausted. Broke. Burnt out. Not in the best headspace.

But she planted a seed.

The job I was in had no opportunity for growth. Coaching seemed simple… and purposeful. Helping people feel better in their bodies? That sounded like me.

I said yes.

My first client was my husband.

Together, we lost a combined 180 pounds, and from there, my business exploded.

Over the next decade, I built a thriving coaching business. I supported clients through weight loss and lifestyle changes and eventually began training other coaches to do the same.

The community I found through this was unlike anything I'd ever known. These weren't just colleagues. They were lifters. Encouragers. Purpose-driven people who wanted others to win.

For the first time, I felt surrounded by people who built each other up, instead of tearing down.

That environment unlocked something in me. Something I didn't know was there.

I discovered I was an entrepreneur.

Me. The girl from the trailer park. The one who had survived abuse, addiction, shame, and suicide ideation.

And the wildest part? My story became part of what grew my business. I started sharing it; raw, unfiltered, real. And people responded. They cried. They messaged me. They told me it gave them hope.

They called me "inspirational."

Me? The girl who dragged herself through the mud of her life?

I still don't know if I believe it.

But I don't hate myself the way I used to.

And that's progress.

The more I succeeded, the more attention I got.

I had to learn how to be seen; a hard shift for someone whose default has always been invisibility. I was used to hiding. Blending in. Playing small.

But the moment that changed everything was when they played a video of my story in front of nearly 20,000 people.

I sat next to my husband in the front row "Reserved Seating", watching my face on the screen, hearing my voice narrate my life; and then I stepped into the spotlight on stage.

Shine, baby, shine.

No more shrinking. No more silence. No more making myself small to make others comfortable.

I still don't love the attention at big events, but I love what my story does.

If it helps someone feel less alone, it's worth *every second*.

I was trying to find my own way out of the dark.

But if my story helps someone else rise as well…

Then all the wounds were worth it.

Chapter 15 Reflection Questions – Becoming Me

1. What identity have you embraced that once felt impossible or out of reach?

2. What has your healing unlocked—not just for you, but for others?

3. What would it look like to stop shrinking and allow yourself to be fully seen?

Chapter Sixteen – The House Faith Built

This new adventure: being a business owner, and the success it brought; gave us what we had dreamed of for years.

We built a house.

After so much financial strain and living in rental homes, we finally had the means to create something permanent. A place where our kids could grow, host their friends, and feel grounded. A space that felt like us.

We broke ground in March 2020, right as the pandemic hit.

We had so much fun choosing every detail and watching it all come together over the course of many months. We visited the site almost daily. The kids called dibs on their rooms, and we let them write their names in Sharpie on the concrete floors. Then, as a family, we covered the home in scripture. Writing verses on the studs and walls and prayed over it room by room.

We paused. Questioned the timing.

Is this wise?

What if we lose our home like we both did after divorce? What if it sinks us again?

But we chose to trust.

To believe that if the doors were opening, it was because God was making a way.

And I'm so glad we did.

If we had waited even one more year, we wouldn't have been able to afford the home we now live in. The market soared. The timing was miraculous.

It wasn't just a house. It was a full-circle moment. A promise kept.

Chapter 16 Reflection Questions – A Home by Faith

1. What dream did survival force you to bury—and are you ready to dig it up again?

2. In what ways has God provided at just the right time in your life?

3. What does "home" mean to you now—and how can you create more of that feeling in your everyday life?

Chapter Seventeen – When the Body Speaks

I finally believed the life ahead of me would be different.

I had hope. I had healing. I was turning 40 and in the best shape of my life.

We celebrated Covid-style, outdoors hiking Tumamoc Hill, releasing butterflies at the top. It was beautiful. Sacred. Symbolic.

Then my body turned on me.

Not physically at first. Mentally.

The work I had done on my health hadn't yet touched the deep-rooted trauma embedded in my nervous system. And when the grief came, it came like an avalanche.

My brother-in-law died of an overdose.

My niece was left parentless, her mom, my sister, still in prison.

Then my sister-in-law took her own life.

Two more children, orphaned.

My brother was incarcerated.

And my youngest brother faced extremely shocking, serious criminal charges and was later convicted.

All of this… in one devastating season.

I relapsed.

Not with drugs, but with alcohol. My old friend. My old escape.

But this time, I didn't let it bury me.

I went back to therapy.

Started asking better questions, about both the physical and emotional roots.

Eventually, I was diagnosed with Complex Post Traumatic Stress Disorder (CPTSD), Pre-Menstrual Dysphoric Disorder (PMDD), and histamine intolerance.

I finally had answers.

And answers gave me something I never had before: options.

I gave up alcohol again—my last drink was May 22, 2022.

I started managing my conditions holistically; and yes, with medication. That part was hard. I rarely even take aspirin. But the difference was undeniable.

For the first time in my life, I felt mentally normal.

But that progress came at a cost.

The weight came back. Fast. Sixty pounds over a few months. I went from my healthiest back to my heaviest—235 pounds.

It was devastating.

But I had to choose:

Do I want a *quiet mind* or a smaller body?

I chose peace.

I could lose weight later. But I couldn't go back to feeling like a prisoner in my own mind.

The medication made me constantly hungry. Weight loss felt impossible.

On top of that, my histamine intolerance ruled out many of the foods I had relied on before.

Eventually, I humbled myself and asked my doctor about a GLP-1. Me—the health coach—asking for help. I felt shame, but I pushed through.

I just started my third week and I'm already down 8 pounds.

Progress.

Last weekend, I went to a coaching event. I almost didn't go.

Everyone's going to see you've gained weight, the enemy whispered.

But I showed up.

And I was greeted with nothing but love.

I shared the new parts of my story. My struggle. My shame. And my people met me with grace.

This is why I love them.

A week before that event, I had gone in for a high-risk breast cancer screening.

My paternal grandmother had breast cancer. Double mastectomy. I had my baseline at 40, and this was the follow-up.

They found a sizable mass on the left side.

I went in for a diagnostic mammogram and an extensive ultrasound.

I waited. And prayed.

The results came back normal.

Thank you, Jesus.

I turned 44 this year—the age my father was when he died. The number has lingered in my mind for years.

When I thought I might have cancer again, it crossed my mind:

Is this how I go?

But not this time.

This chapter isn't just about illness or weight.

It's about choosing to keep showing up.

Even when the fear is loud.

Even when your reflection changes.

Even when the old voices try to pull you under.

You still rise.

Chapter 17 Reflection Questions – When the Body Speaks

1. When has your body or mind forced you to pause and pay attention—whether through illness, exhaustion, or breakdown?

2. Have you ever felt shame for needing help? What would it look like to trade that shame for compassion?

3. What's one way you can honor your body today—not for how it looks, but for how it has carried you through?

Chapter Eighteen – Rescuer, Wounded

Right before Halloween 2020, we moved into our new home.

A couple months later, we all got Covid.

While we were quarantined, a call came about a child relative. DCS had removed her from the home. We offered to help, temporarily. To give her stability, love, and a chance for her parents to get back on their feet.

As soon as quarantine lifted, she came to live with us.

We became licensed foster parents soon after.

What followed was one of the hardest years of our lives.

I won't share her story. But I will say this:

Every time someone blamed the lack of support or resources on "Covid," I wanted to scream.

We had to disrupt the placement.

We were in over our heads, and no one cared.

The transition was traumatic; for the child, and for us. The process was deeply flawed. We struggled to find the support we needed, and despite advocating through every channel we could, it felt like no one was listening.

We were so heartbroken; we closed our license.

We knew we couldn't do it again.

I used my voice. I tried to shake the system. But no one moved.

Covid also impacted my health in other ways.

I ended up in the ER with heart arrhythmia and shortness of breath.

The symptoms stuck around. I still have the arrhythmia. Running became impossible—that gutted me. I had run multiple 5Ks, half marathons, and even a full marathon in 2015.

Now, I could barely breathe.

I wore a heart monitor for a few weeks. They observed it, but ultimately said it was within the normal range.

Hallelujah.

It still hasn't fully resolved, but it's manageable.

We tried to help.

And we paid for it.

But even in the heartbreak, I believe we were part of her rescue.

Even if it was only for a season.

Chapter 18 Reflection Questions – Rescuer, Wounded

1. When have you said "yes" to helping someone and later realized you were in over your head? What did you learn about your limits?

2. What grief do you carry from trying to do the right thing in a broken system?

3. How can you give yourself permission to let go of guilt for what you couldn't control?

Chapter Nineteen – Starting Again

After the pandemic, my coaching business began to decline.

It had been my primary income for years; our livelihood, really; and suddenly it wasn't enough. I knew I needed something else to fill the gap financially. I wasn't thrilled about going back into property management, but that's where most of my experience was.

I started applying.

Hundreds of applications. Months of silence. Despite over two decades in that industry, I only got a few interviews; and mostly polite rejections. That was it.

I realized quickly that the job market had changed, and for the first time, I didn't have a connection to help get me in the door.

I decided to expand my search beyond rentals and stumbled across a position for a Community Association Manager. A.K.A. Homeowners Associations.

Ugh.

I had always looked down on HOA work. I saw it as the bottom of the industry. The job no one wanted. But of course, that's the role that called me back. That's the one that offered me the job.

"You're funny, God," I remember thinking. "Where are you leading me?"

Still, I said yes. I chose to trust.

Fast forward two years, and I'm still here.

It's a great company. I love my team. Best of all, there's real potential for growth.

I continue to coach, in the nooks and crannies of my day. Rebuilding it would take serious time and energy; and I haven't yet decided what that might look like. But I know I'll always be connected to that mission. In some way, coaching will always be part of my life.

This new job has allowed me to dream again.

Health issues and financial shifts made the last few years hard. They made me question myself. But now? I feel possibility again.

We've started talking about what's next.

Once the younger kids are grown, we plan to leave Arizona. I've grown to appreciate the desert, but it's not my happy place. I want green, water, ocean air, real seasons.

Our kids can stay or go with us, but either way, this won't be our forever. We'll likely keep the house here, maybe rent it to the children if that works out.

We've been scouting possible landing spots.

Our best friends moved to Virginia Beach last summer, definitely an option.

Then there's Hawaii. My husband spent part of his childhood on Oahu, and it's always called to him. Last year, he surprised me with a quick birthday trip to Waikiki. It was everything.

Naturally, I looked up job opportunities—and wouldn't you know it? They're hiring. And they pay well.

Add it to the list.

My husband still carries a desire in his heart; to live internationally. He almost moved after his divorce but stayed for his kids. I'm grateful he did. We never would have met otherwise.

I asked him recently, "Where would you go if it were entirely up to you?"

He said, "London."

Straight to UK job boards I went. Guess what? They have HOAs there too.

Now, we're excited. Planning. Watching the next season start to unfold.

We have a few years yet until our youngest is grown—but it feels good to *look forward* again.

Chapter 19 Reflection Questions – The Door You Didn't Expect

1. Have you ever walked through a door you didn't want to open—only to find purpose or peace on the other side?

2. What dreams have reawakened in you recently? What would it look like to give yourself permission to pursue them?

3. If you could live anywhere in the next season of life, where would you go—and who would you become there?

Chapter Twenty – What Helped Me Heal

Here are the practices and truths that helped me rebuild. I don't share these as prescriptions, but as invitations.

Before I close, I want to leave you with *something real*.

Tangible. Practical. Raw.

These are things that helped me crawl out of the pit. Things I still lean on today.

1. God.

If you don't know Him yet, start there.

Cry out.

Admit you're a sinner (we all are).

Believe in Jesus.

Accept that He died for you.

Then commit your life to Him.

That's it. Simple, but life-altering.

If you already know God and you've walked far away?

He's still there. Still loves you.

Like us loving our kids, even when they mess up.

2. Mindset is everything.

Your thoughts create your reality.

I had to do a lot of work here, my beliefs around money, parenting, marriage, faith, self-worth.

Add in that three of our four kids are neurodivergent. It has been HARD. But learning how they think, how they receive love, how they need to be supported. It changed everything.

Give yourself grace.

None of us know what we're doing. We're all winging it with the best of intentions.

3. Find your people.

Make a list of qualities you want in a friend.

Then go where people like that gather.

Get in the rooms.

Join the community.

Be the beginner.

4. Go to therapy.

Period.

5. Own your own shit.

You can't heal if you keep blaming everyone else.

Shift from victim to victor.

Grow in emotional intelligence. Learn how to regulate your feelings so you can lead with intention, not reactivity.

6. Get curious about your behavior.

Awareness is the beginning of change.

Don't beat yourself up. Ask why.

7. Be resourceful.

Read. Study. Research.

The answers are out there.

8. Ask for help.

Find a mentor.

Watch how they live.

Ask questions.

Let them coach you through the things they've already walked out.

9. Love well.

Life is short. Don't waste it chasing *counterfeit love*.

And if you're a believer, don't marry a non-believer. I learned that the hard way. Scripture is clear, and for good reason.

10. Advocate for your health.

If something feels off, get it checked.

If a doctor dismisses you, find another one.

PMDD wrecked my life for years, and no one took me seriously. I was told I was dramatic. Emotional. "Just hormonal."

It wasn't until I got answers that I got relief.

11. Live a healthy lifestyle.

This was the starting point of all my healing.

Stop eating crap. Drink water. Move your body.

You don't have to be perfect. Just start.

If you need help, I'm here as a resource.

12. Healing prayer changed my life.

If you've never gone through a healing prayer session, do it.

Sever soul ties. Reclaim territory the enemy tried to steal.

There's real power in calling it all by name and releasing it.

And finally…REMEMBER:

You are not what happened to you.

You are not where you came from.

You are not the worst thing you've done.

You are not your trauma.

You *can* create something beautiful.

You *can* rewrite your story.

Will it be hard? Yes.

Will it be worth it? Absolutely.

No one can fight for your healing but you.

But you are worth the fight.

I'm still healing. Still growing. Still becoming. And so are you.

Chapter 20 Reflection Questions – What I Know Now

1. What have you learned about healing that you wish someone had told you sooner?

2. Where are you still tempted to shrink or hide your story? What would happen if you shared it more boldly?

3. Which of the truths shared in this chapter speaks most to you right now—and what's one way you can live it out today?

Appendix – Mentioned Conditions Explained

CPTSD is like PTSD, but it's caused by long-term or repeated trauma, especially from childhood or relationships.

People with CPTSD often deal with:

- Flashbacks or nightmares from past trauma
- Always feeling on edge or like danger is around the corner
- Emotional numbness or shutting down to protect themselves
- Low self-worth or deep shame
- Trouble with relationships or trusting others
- Big emotional reactions or feeling out of control sometimes

Unlike PTSD, which can develop from a single traumatic event (like a car accident), CPTSD builds over time, especially if the person couldn't escape the situation.

Healing is possible, but it takes effort. Treatment often includes therapy focused on rebuilding safety, emotional regulation, and self-worth.

PMDD is like PMS (premenstrual syndrome), but much more intense.

Each month before a woman's cycle, hormone changes can trigger symptoms like:

- Severe mood swings
- Feeling very sad, angry, or anxious
- Fatigue, brain fog, or trouble sleeping
- Physical symptoms like bloating or breast tenderness

But with PMDD, these symptoms are so strong that they affect daily life, work, relationships, and mental health. Some women even feel depressed or have thoughts of self-harm during this time.

The symptoms usually start in the week or two before the period and go away shortly after it begins.

It's a real medical condition—far more than just 'being emotional.' Treatment can include lifestyle changes, therapy, medication, or hormonal options to help balance things out.

Histamine intolerance happens when your body has too much histamine; a natural chemical involved in digestion, immune response, and even brain function; but can't break it down fast enough.

Histamine is found in many foods, especially things like:

- Aged cheese, smoked meats, and fermented foods
- Wine and alcohol
- Vinegar, tomatoes, and spinach
- Leftovers or anything that's been sitting a while

If your body can't handle the histamine load (usually because of a deficiency in the enzyme DAO, which breaks it down), you might get symptoms like:

- Headaches or migraines
- Rashes, itching, or hives
- Nasal congestion or asthma-like symptoms
- Stomach issues (bloating, nausea, cramps, diarrhea)
- Anxiety or dizziness
- Irregular periods or hormone imbalance

It can mimic a food allergy, but it's not the immune system reacting—it's a build-up issue.

Managing it usually means changing your diet, avoiding high-histamine foods, and sometimes taking supplements like DAO or antihistamines. It's often tricky to diagnose, so working with a knowledgeable provider is key.

PMDD and histamine intolerance are connected through shared pathways involving estrogen, inflammation, and nervous system dysregulation, all of which can be affected by past trauma.

Estrogen naturally fluctuates throughout the menstrual cycle. Rising estrogen stimulates the release of histamine and also suppresses DAO, the enzyme responsible for clearing it. This can lead to excess histamine in the body, and histamine, in turn, can increase estrogen activity, creating a feedback loop that heightens hormone sensitivity.

When trauma is present, particularly chronic or early-life trauma, the nervous system may remain in a heightened state of alert. This dysregulated stress response (often seen in CPTSD) can impair the body's ability to process both hormones and inflammatory signals like histamine. Trauma can also impact gut health, which plays a key role in breaking down both histamine and estrogen.

In people with PMDD, who are already sensitive to hormonal changes, this layered effect, trauma, histamine buildup, and hormone reactivity, can amplify the body's response to natural shifts in the cycle.

In short: Trauma can dysregulate the nervous system and gut, which reduces the body's ability to clear histamine and balance hormones. Since estrogen increases histamine and histamine enhances estrogen's effects, the result is a compounding cycle that worsens PMDD in those with histamine intolerance.

Author Bio

Salina Watson is a writer, speaker, worship singer, and leader whose life story is a powerful testimony of resilience, redemption, and faith. A survivor of childhood trauma, addiction, and family dysfunction, Salina rose from broken beginnings to build a life rooted in healing, purpose, and hope.

She spent over two decades in property and community management while also leading a nationally recognized health coaching business that impacted thousands. Known for her raw honesty and compassionate voice, Salina empowers others to confront their past, find their voice, and believe in the possibility of transformation.

Salina lives in Arizona with her husband and four children. When she's not writing or mentoring, you can find her near the ocean, dreaming of coastal life and helping others shine through the shadows.

Acknowledgments

First, to God: my ever-present help in every storm. You have never left me. Even in the darkest places, You were there, gently calling me back to life.

To my husband: thank you for loving me through every chapter, even the ones I hadn't yet healed from. Your steady strength, quiet faith, and deep love have been a safe place for me to grow, rebuild, and shine. You were an answered prayer I didn't know how to ask for.

To my children: thank you for giving me a reason to fight harder, love deeper, and heal more honestly. You are the legacy I dreamed of. May you always know that your story matters.

To the friends who became family: your encouragement, prayers, and presence sustained me when I felt like quitting. Thank you for holding space for my truth, for calling out the gold in me, and for reminding me who I am when I forget.

To my mentors, coaches, and leaders: you helped me step into purpose when I still saw myself as broken. Thank you for creating spaces where healing was possible and for teaching me how to lead with integrity and heart.

To those who hurt me: you became the backdrop of the redemption story. God used it all. And I am no longer bound by bitterness.

Dear Reader,

Thank you for walking through these pages with me.

This wasn't an easy book to write, and I imagine some parts weren't easy to read either. But if you made it here, to the end, I want you to know something:

You matter.

Your story matters.

Whether you've walked through similar shadows, or your path has been completely different, I hope you felt seen. I hope you found pieces of light in the cracks of my story that reflected something in your own.

This book isn't just about me. It's about all of us who have survived what was meant to break us and chose to keep going anyway.

You don't have to be perfect. You don't have to have it all figured out. You're allowed to be in process. You're allowed to still be healing. And even if no one else has ever told you this—I'm proud of you.

Thank you for giving me your time, your trust, and your presence here.

I pray that as you move forward, you'll carry this truth with you:

You are not too far gone. And you don't have to walk through the dark alone.

With love and light,
Salina Watson

Let's Stay Connected

If this book spoke to your heart, I would love to hear from you.

You can connect with me on social media, share your story, or just say hello. It means more than you know to walk this journey with others who are healing, growing, and rising too.

Instagram: @salinacwatson
Facebook: Salina Watson
Email: shinethroughtheshadowswithme@gmail.com

Tag me when you post or share the book; I would love to cheer you on.

And if this story touched you, consider leaving a review. It helps other readers find the light as well.

Made in the USA
Coppell, TX
04 December 2025